Me and My Thoughts

Aaliah Malik

BookLeaf
Publishing

India | USA | UK

Presentation by *BookLeaf Publishing*

Web: www.bookleafpub.com

E-mail: info@bookleafpub.com

ISBN: 9789357691727

First edition 2022

State Of Mind

I writhe in my skin
Fear rising within
If those guys are out again
Then I'll be hiding in
My room
Cos no matter what I'm avoiding
Danger at all costs, I got no wish of dying
These thoughts are blinding
So these words are binding
And even when you can identify this there's no
finding
A way out,
And if you see me crying
Its not you, its just strangers, you say you want
me to dive in
To an explanation of how I'm feeling
But that'll take way too long to explain without
leaving
Out key details, plus I hate speaking
I stumble over my words, my breathing
Becomes unsteady
Legs are shaky
Even when I ready
Cos these thoughts are heavy
My vision gets blurry
My eyes are filling with tears

You didn't hurt me
Its just because now I'm letting all the worry
Take over my body and that's cos there is no
stopping
It now
At least that's what I'm convinced is true, you
say you disagree, I don't understand but how
Cos my head is filled with ideas most foul
And they're not even real, irrational fears, I
shout
In their face, but they still chase me around
Honestly, I kinda believe that there's no getting
out,
As they scowl
At me whenever I try and drown
Myself or my doubt
In my house
I hear sounds
That will cloud
My thoughts
And there's no coming round
Back from this insanity
I've crowned me a worthy queen,
but weak , failure , so firstly I decree
That nobody will ever be able to see me crying
In pain, never again, no one will see me
Struggling, you say ive given up but trust me I'm
trying

I don't like
my state of mind
I lie to my-
-self then I expect me to be fine

Pessimist

I've got a feeling that something is gonna go
wrong
I don't know what it is Something just feels so
off
It just scares me that I don't know what's going
on
I know I should relax but my mind just wont
stop

It's as though i tripped
fell over the edge of a cliff
Tryna hold on but now I'm starting to slip
Its startling to think
That if I can't keep my grip
Then I'll fall And I'll hit
The ground, and my head
Will violently split
In to two and my limbs -
shattered
My bones crumbling
I'm suffering
In silence
yeah this imagery is vile and
Unpleasant but it's my
way of explaining my state Of mind

And my current state of life
I know it's all down to nights
Lying awake and almost crying
Over the past and also fighting
with the future I've been writing,
I know it's false, though it's not right it's
So believable, so inviting

Move On

You can't run very far with all that on your back
So lighten your load or your spine will crack
and snap in half
why would you make it so hard
harder than it needs to be
You've really gotta start
to carry around less of your past
cos what's done was done, but now you've got to
last
until the end
so You've gotta make room for your fast paced
race against the clock,
Till the times up never stop

never fall back
they may talk bad
but don't back down for that
You might get mad
just stay on your track
And it'll get better I'll put anything on that

because you're better than
you have ever let
yourself believe
never forget that

you're better than when
you did all that back then
put it behind you
forgive and forget

So put that bag down
that you've been carrying around
it weighs more than you,
And it's been dragging you down
Stop allowing yourself to drown in a pool
of what was,
focus on what is, and what if,
don't drive yourself off the edge of that cliff
cos there's so much more to you I see,
and I still
Won't let you go till you see the same as me -
and you will

Lost Myself

Stepping out in front of these people
so im stressing now,
What are they thinking? I'm desperately tryna
figure out
what's going through their minds when they see
me,
guessing south is where this is going
So I'm breathing loud
And my chest is heaving - ow
Pushing aside all the hope only believing doubt
that has clouded my thoughts
but there's no leaving now
I try to shout but what I speak isn't coming out!

The pressure's on, but im pressing on
Plan on impressing all of the people who are
gawping at me as i talk
And although I may be short
I feel so tall compared to those who are gazing
towards
me
And its almost unfazing when my thoughts
freeze,
cos I was expecting this ,
Can I take a call please?

No - I don't get a break cos there's no pausing
this fight with my amygdala,
cos, man, we're brawling

Stronger Than Ever

Stepping into the ring for the fight of the century
I'm only here to win, and with delight they will
mention me
In their little stories, I think I make quite an
entry
Blasting eminem as I walk towards my destiny
with all those heavy punches I admit I'm quite a
sight to see
I won't be running from this Cos i know that in
some time I'll be
the greatest to ever grace this place, here, with
their presence
Don't believe me? Come and fight with me -
you punch slower than i can sight-read
Adrenaline pumping through my veins
Like I'm pedaling
Away from the chains
of an evil that chases
All its prey
till it presses the breaks
and falls in disgrace
But the difference it makes
To have all my faith
And ability to make all fall into place
Not to mention, my pace

Man im winning this race

I'm back and I'm stronger than ever
I feel like a winner
I'm back and I'm better
Better late than never

Carnage

At first sight of me
you may be averse to me
but it just takes a verse to be
made certain I'm an adversary
And I'm on the verge of being
merged into a world of hurt
Not just for me but for the rest of the earth
cos ive unearthed a curse
that may burn the worst
Wounds,
And these words
Are no exaggeration but an understatement
of what I have to offer
and this ain't no vile (vial) in which you can put
a stopper
And your life, like me, will only grow tougher
Cos in my eyes, what I see is, you were all born
to suffer
before you're able to find shelter to hide under
cos you can't finish strong without beginning at
the bottom

Yadda Yadda Yadda

Yadda yadda yadda
Man the words I gotta under-
stand, eyes are flicking up and
Down so I don't miss a thing
brother imma punch ya
If you don't stop and shut ya
Babbling-bogus gob up
Because what you utter gives me nausea

And there ain't a single other
Rapper singer or a tougher
Composer who can give ya
All this fire and maintain composure
Under pressure
Not a poser
I'll bet ya
Can't get over
My talent with the
Pro type
Lyricism and the total
Brutal honesty in what i say
You run for me, cos some will blame
Me for their problems but truth is they're just
plain lame

Cos they don't understand that this is a two lane
game
So theyre biased and only have one idea of who
they'll shame
But my name, is one so great no one can claim,
it Nor my face
I won't ever be an object that you use to gain
fame
Yeah I will yell at you with no end, if you try put
me in chains
Cos I'm on a train, and it's destination is one
that's gated,
But does that mean I'll reach heaven or hell, well
I can't say,
Its, dependant on how Im spending, this
seemingly never ending,
And bumpy and bending, journey, my fate's still
pending...
I'm learning, much more about me, I hope my
life ain't ending

Influence

Sometimes we sit back and wonder
'Do i deserve to have much longer
in this world, in this life' and all the
Things we fear seem to grasp and take over
our emotions
the flow of the notions
In our brains,
and opposing all our opinions is statements
made
By the people in the media
And blocking it out ain't getting any easier
Cos the number of people being influenced has
raised
Their minds being swayed in one way and now
they cant be saved
Because the paths been paved
So now they follow it,
blindly, and it can't be changed
But the art we make
It will start to take
A toll on their minds so then their hearts will
change
And no matter how far back we are in this race
The strength of our minds will help us pick up
the pace

The Fame Game

Those who you idolise will affect your character
So don't look up to people presented by a
caricature
Cos they'll fool you
And then you'll be lured to become who they
are, thinking that they are a perfectly good dude
When in reality
Their best value is their fortune
So don't copy those with fame
Only sing along to your tune
Cos theres people who will fake it till they make
it
Then steal your heart and ache it till they break
it
So let's face it
You cant trust the biggest faces
The biggest names tend to have the image which
is fakest
So don't fall for it
Look up to those who dont just talk for in-
-valuable gain and the attention,
its insane
how much some of these people will change
for the cameras, for validation from their fan
base

and man its left a bad taste
so I'm disgusted by these sad traits
why won't they just be genuine, I can't place
my finger on it
what are their reasons
whyre they so desperate that they're acting
when they're not working, they're off set,
but they use what their drama teacher said
they stay in character and never turn their heads
to us,
its an impressive part
But an intensive task
So pretentious, they cant forget the past
but must have regrets but pass
those to the next, who'll ask
"should I be true to myself or not
should I deceive and plot,
or stay pristine, or just hope to never be caught"
Its an unfortunate cycle
yet we're tricked by them despite know-ing
that the ones before made us believe they were
likable
Maybe we're part of this, partly responsible
for why it doesn't stop cos
their roles played are easily recyclable
we know they're masks, but they're so inviting
though

Prisoner

I'm not allowed outside cos I've done a lotta
work to keep me behind bars, I'm gonna wanna
leave soon, but I strive to go and call on all the
things that make me feel glued to the dark of all
the
things that I've done, but I'm cutting off ties
So I've got my top button undone, and I find
That hurting those who have hurt you most will
burn the most anger the fumes will curl your
toes,
Inside
I'm a mess of lies and doubts that bind
to my best of lines that convince me I'm fine
and i just wanna remind you all that im kind
enough to give myself time to fight
back before I pick up the knife and end it all
with a swift swipe, slicing
my throat, but I'm liking
the struggle, though it's my sin
I'm also my own victim
And this all links in
to why I'm the way I am;
the overthinkng
and all the sinking into made up frustrating
situations

Why there's no hesitation with self-deprecation
Its an indication that I should be taking
medication
But whatever, I'll be fine ...
Its just a phase...isn't it?
The infiltration of the ways of other people my
age!

SMILE

Its my cerebral disease yeah my insanity
And unequal degrees of feelings inside of me
And the people that leave when I'm inclined to
weep
They're the evil that refuel my will to write and
speak
Rope round my throat is tightening
Yet I still cope and fight the things
That make me feel like I dont deserve the wings
That'll help me fly and say goodbye to my
suffering
Another thing is that I have this bubbling
Anger inside me, muffling its mumbling
About all my fumbling
When I'm struggling
To speak to people cos I shudder in
The presence of those who with which I can't be
comforted
And as some put it
I'm incompetent so now it's time for this
Breakthrough in the system like a cyber glitch
Straight through the lit entrance I'm a fighter,
kids!
And now none of you will hide from this
Cos when I go seek I know that I will win

Cos I'm like a giant in
This place full of small minded insolent
Little irritant people who spit
Man its such a shame to live in the world that I
live in
Cos I'm higher than
Everyone else cos I'm inspiring
While they're conspiring
About firing off at those who know the truth
about their snipering
And its frightening
How they buy their win
With the money they've made from their heist to
spin
The tables round to make it seem like they're the
fighters in
This place when really they're the lying winners

Fight Your Demons

My rise and fall
With my mic I talk
Don't like to bore
You with lies or false
Claims, try to pour
My heart and soul into these thoughts
I hope you all
Will take a minute to pause
And actually think about the words
That im saying cos I was taught
By legends how to draw
A picture in a listeners mind
Present core beliefs
Intense struggles, relief
From the tugging ropes that your mind has tied
to your feet!

And how to help you receive
A sense of comfort and feel
Like you're not alone and you can be
Anything you dream
And have everything you need
To succeed by just being
Yourself and not seeking
Validation from the evil
People who have no meaning

In their hatred, what they're seeing
Is your few flaws, their sight is leaving
Cos they cant see when your strong
Feeding
Into your doubt
I'm Pleading
That you're
Thinking about yourself, no one else cos they
won't help
Their opinions they won't sell
They're the ones who deserve hell
So be present, don't be a shell
Hollowed out by fears of future spells
Of failure, just focus on what's going on right
now, right here
You're gonna be ok, the light is near
So fight your tears
In spite of this
State of constant pain and now your peers
Will help you through it all not just your career
Your path to freedom will be cleared
And the sound of cheers, can you hear it?
Our minds were blackened now we've cleaned
em
The ropes' grasps have slackened so we leave
them
To be burned we're heathen
But We're even more religious despite our
demons

Long Road

I can even hear my own heart beating
In my chest, and im not feeling
All too great but I cant start feeding
Into my worries, or my chest will start heaving
And I'm not leaving
These thoughts behind
I'm just taking a break
Tryna organise my mind
A little better, cos sometimes
It gets too messy, and causes my stressing
But I can sweep away the dirt, and with a little
time
And I can start to feel better
Achieve medals, eventually start to stop
dreading
Every possible moment I'll have to be
conversing
With someone else
By learning, that doing it will help
my mental health
My internal doubt
That scours round my bound
Brain and batters down my crown
Till its in pieces
No, until its powdered down

Hear the fear in my voice, see my tears, when I
shout
Don't want my screams to get out
But its seems i fell out
Of my seat, wheres my belt
Its torn apart its no use now
Tryna save me from hell
Think I can hear the alarum bell
I fear I will be quelled
But I have so much still to tell

Acceptance

Living high on life
Killing strife all night
Winning prize, that's right
Spending time, on my
Mental state, and my minds
Strength when it comes to fights,
Bent out of shape, but I'll find
A way to make it work for my
Way of thinking, and how I go about dealing
With different problems, I ain't leaving
Them behind, I'll be linking
Myself to ask those inklings
I was feeling when I was in a state of grieving
I'm not alright, but I'm trying, to make the climb
To the sky,
I can't deny that i cry, myself to sleep
sometimes,
But now I'm doing that less, so I must be doing
something right
Im starting to think im fine
I've never even wanted to die

But sometimes I shy away from the day
Yeah sometimes I'm inclined to ignore those
who say

"You gotta talk to people if you wanna try and make
Yourself some friends, you can't just sit there and play
With ur pen and ruler for the whole hour, in every lesson,
How can you go the
Whole year not talking
To anyone else in your classroom?"
I hear them but don't listen
I give bigger issues my attention
I know the reason I don't talk is cos Im socially anxious
Yeah cos when I speak out loud you don't know what im risking
Cos I swear if I slip up out of that door I will be sprinting
And the scared thoughts that focus on the teared parts of my heart are lingering
Even if the world was war free, I'd still see blood glistening

Battle Scars Are Victory Marks

There's certain things I say
That'll never see the light of day
I think I'll have a fight today
So can you go and light the way
Ready my chariot, I like to make
A statement on entering, oh fie the wave
Of supporters for the so called brave
Opponent, but dont leave, just wait
He's already one foot in the grave
So just wait see, I swear that you'll be pleased
When i go out there and show em what a wonder
i am to see
I'm undefeated
I can't be cheated
Fans can't remain seated
They stand up and exclaim "beat him"
Even if I have no reason
To inflict pain on the opposition
My instinct says don't be a like a pigeon
Be an eagle, be a hawk, be the predator, make
him stop
In his tracks, overcome by fear
Then envelop him in your wings, and then your
ears will be met with cheers
You'll be the very one that they revere

I Can't Get Away

Crippling fear
Rippling tears
Sifting and filtering all of your peers
Clicking the gears
Tricking the chase
Flipping and flickering every switch
Gripping the praise
Hitting the waves
Swishing and twisting you down to your grave
Pity the craze
Ridding the gaze
Scaring and staring at all in its trails

This world will amaze
This girl is unfazed
I can't be complaining or I'll lose my praise
They say its a faze
But it stays everyday
They can't be correct cos they're crushing my
faith
I can't get away
Yeah I can't escape

We Need Answers (Part 1)

Living in a world where we love our neighbour
Living in a world where we rely on one another
Hit 'em with a curse so they'll take cover
Rid 'em of their pearls so they sink under
In confusion
Your delusion
Has made the world struggle, your illusion
Is a fusion
Of evil and intrusion
Into the minds of the youthful
Not useful, but you shoot full
Barrels of bullets, they ricochet off the derelict
Houses and it rouses, the people who still have
the prowess and the powers, cast showers
Upon those who dry up rivers and burn flowers
Knock towers, down till they're nought but
powder
How'd the guilty get away with these pesky
And these reckless actions
Without facing any sanctions
At least retract them
From the rest of us who are
Frightened, enlightened about how we might end
up dying

We Need Answers (Part 2)

Livin in a world where we feel safe under covers
Livin in a world where you're father says your
brothers toughest
Stick em in a hearse so they can't be prophets
Spit until they hurl themselves headfirst into a
coffin

Cos you polluted
Their brain
And your name and place is rooted
From an ancient plane
Where people burnt civilians for their individual
beliefs
Caused them strife as if their life were on an
ending lease
And they begged "Sir Please
We are bleeding, just reading about what we
seek in
Living in a society
Where the dictator feels he's a deity
But really, in his entirety
He's nothing more then a smudge on a papyrus
sheet"

He has a liars teeth

There's gaps, they're broken,
Servants didn't meet his dire needs
Exactly as he decreed
Yet he doesn't seem to see how what he speaks is
what bleeds
Blood thats black, not red he makes all blue
This the truth, is what's been hidden
From the innocent,
When they seek help from you

You're Wrong About Me

So..
I'm tryna make it clear that I dont need to fit in
For me to end up being the one doing the
winning
Cos you and I we're not alike, Cos unlike you
I've thick skin
And i will end the hardest fights that you could
only begin

Life's harder than you think
And that you try to make it seem
You wouldn't take a hit for your team
You'd dodge a bullet, let it reach
Its target
Even if it was your father,
Your mother or your brother
Either way you wouldn't bother
Just as long as you don't suffer

And I want you to know I look down you
And there's nowhere to go, except a garbage
chute
That's where you belong, wanna know what I'm
gonna do?

Imma hit every target you said I could never
shoot!

Buzzing
God I feel free
Fly like a butterfly
Sting like a bee
I'm on another high
You can't even see me
You're like Sonny Liston
Against me, Muhammed Ali !

Copycat

Why do you follow me
Why d'you keep copying me
Why d'you always bother me
Don't say ur a friend I see

That you're obsessive we
Cannot be friends it seems
You don't wanna be you so just try and mirror
the

Things that I say and do
You're making you look like a fool
I don't how to to tell you all of this without
sounding cruel

But truth is, and I'll prove this,
Its better if you lose this
Dubious and peculiar
Tendency, it's not a cute touch

I don't like it when you repeat what I recite and
say I like
But I don't fight, it cos if I did, then you would
just, despite it,

Carry on and deny that what you do is a pain,
light it
Up and fuel the blaze that just thrives so I'm
reminded

Constantly of this giant, and irritating situation
And I'm just tired, can't be asked to lie, I'm
impatient
And sympathy is long gone for you, In actuality
I'm back to see how you've changed in all this
insanity

Can You Hear Me?

Can you hear me?
Cos it feels like no one is listening
Even when I'm shouting and screaming
My chest is heaving
And I feel like I'm struggling with my breathing

Its so deceiving
When I'm smiling when out on the street and
All my feelings are bottled up within me
And I'm bleeding, and no one knows it's eating
me raw from the inside

It feels like
I'm starting to die away
Eventhough I'm far from my final day
I'm not okay
I've had this feeling before but now it won't go
away

I'm starting to cry all night
I don't sleep, though I'm tired
That therapist I hired
Is no good, now she's fired
They're all liars
They're not fighters

My brain needs to be rewired

Tell me can you see, can you really see me or
Am I invisible, does no one know I'm here?
Tell me can you hear, can you hear the growing
fear
That makes my voice sound weak, d'you go deaf
when I speak?

www.ingramcontent.com/pod-product-compliance
Lightning Source LLC
La Vergne TN
LVHW051241200726
843510LV00011B/1646